If nature had but one song to sing,
each verse would be of beauty.

J. M. Greene

Great Egret

DANCING FEATHERS

Great Egrets

Roseate Spoonbill

Dancing
FEATHERS

Photographs & Reflections
of Wading Birds from
Southern Swamps, Ponds and Rookeries

PHOTOGRAPHS AND TEXT BY
JANIE MOORE GREENE

SEALE PUBLISHING COMPANY
SEALE, ALABAMA

Copyright © 1995 by Janie M. Greene

Library of Congress Cataloging-in-Publication Data
Greene, Janie M., 1995
        Dancing Feathers / Janie Moore Greene -
        First Edition 1995
        Second Edition 1996
        Bibliography

Text edited by Linda Tomblin
Design Consultant, Ed Symmes
Computer layout, Connie Romanishan
Produced 486/Windows using Adobe Photoshop, Quark Xpress, Nikon
Coolscan Slidescanner.

This 1996 edition published and produced by
SAN 298-2714
Seale Publishing Company, P.O. Box 65, Seale, AL 36875
Tel: 334-855-2772 Fax: 334-855-2767

ISBN 0-96415-701-2 Hardcover
        0-9641570-0-4 Paperback
Library of Congress Catalog Card Number 94-92095

Printed in Singapore

Flamingos

ACKNOWLEDGEMENTS

I would like to express sincere appreciation to those who helped me compile this book DANCING FEATHERS:

First of all, my deep gratitude goes to my gentle and kind friend, Linda Tomblin, who faithfully encouraged and organized me. She often collaborated and prayed with me as we worked on the text. Without Linda, DANCING FEATHERS would never have been started or completed.

My sincere appreciation also goes to my mother, Loretta Moore, and my minister, Dr. Gilbert Ramsey, for their valuable critiques on the text,

To Marion Motley Carchache who helped me with grammar,

To Anne Guilfoyle who encouraged and helped me select photographs that would keep me true to the title DANCING FEATHERS, and

To Pat Caulfield who introduced me to the beauty of Nature Photography and the dancing birds of the Everglades.

I am forever grateful to my friends who constantly encouraged me during the two years it took to complete this project, especially Betty Persons and Judy Jackson who did more than their share.

To Eddie Symmes, Connie Romanishan, Frennie Rathel, Dorothy Gibson and Donna Brown who assisted with book design, and

To instructors John Shaw, John Netherton, Patricia Caulfield, Heather Angel, David Middleton, Kathy Bushue, Renee Lynn, and Helen Longest-Slaughter, for giving me their expert advice at Nature Photography Workshops.

Last on this list, but forever first in my heart, I want to thank my beautiful and loving family; Roy, Lynne, Katie, Leslie Anne, Mitch, Sandy, Roy III, Ashley, Dan, Leslie, John Daniel, David, Rosanna, Muriel, Leslie, & Juan, for their patience and willingness to give up their wife, mother and grandmother to allow me to complete the biggest project of my life. And finally my deepest gratitude goes to my Heavenly Father who faithfully guided, directed and empowered me during the creation of DANCING FEATHERS.

Great Blue Heron

DEDICATION

I dedicate this book with deep appreciation to my husband, Roy Greene; for it was he who first conceived the idea and believed that I could write a book. With faithfulness and patience, he has always encouraged and supported me in my interests of writing and nature photography.

American White Pelicans

Great Egret

Reddish Egret

INTRODUCTION

The photographs and most of the essays in this book are combined journal excerpts from several photographic expeditions I made into southern swamps, ponds, and rookeries. These birds are some of the most beautiful and graceful creatures on earth. Known to bird lovers as "waders", they include the Snowy Egret, the Blue Heron, the Roseate Spoonbill, and others too numerous to mention. Brilliant in plumage, graceful in flight, serene in repose, these birds congregate by the hundreds in these rookeries (breeding grounds for different species of birds) where one is afforded an unparalleled opportunity to observe them in their natural habitat.

I began these photographic trips at a time when I was filled with self doubt and too scattered to even know my name. Breaking the pattern of my life, I, who for the past thirty-seven years of marriage never ventured far from home unless I was on the arm of my husband, suddenly decided to go to a photography workshop in the Everglades. Photographing the birds beside Patricia Caulfield, a talented female nature photographer, changed my life. I discovered my bliss and became a passionate bird and nature photographer.

After that, each time I left one photographic expedition tired and exhausted, I couldn't wait for the next one to begin. I was like a person driven, trying to catch up with the years of undeveloped skill, and learn more about nature photography. Oftentimes my husband joined me. He encouraged me, and repeatedly helped me get some of my best photographs, especially when I had to approach the rookery from a boat. Most of the time, the nesting areas were in swamp-like areas surrounded by water and patrolled by alligators.

Peering through the lens of my camera and focusing on the beauty of nature gave me unexpected rewards. I learned and re-learned many lessons in life that emphasized values I'd long cherished, such as loyalty, beauty, simplicity, balance, patience, and growth according to life's rhythms.

In taking the time for solitude there in the primordial swamps, I did more than learn about nature. In the many beautiful scenes coming to me each day, I experienced nature and God's presence in it. It gave me a greater understanding of my individuality, brought the fragmented parts of myself together, and helped me realize the importance of the individuality of all persons. I was able to deal with my many problems by surrendering them to God and came away with a greater love of His creation and His marvelous gift of Himself to others and me through that creation.

Roseate Spoonbill & Willets

NATURE'S PATTERN

Great Blue Herons

NATURE'S PATTERN

The air is cool late this May at my Alabama home. I'm glad because it gives me extra energy before the humid days of summer begin. The fragrance of gardenias from the vase beside my desk fills the room as I look outside the window on plate-sized white magnolia blossoms nestled in the green leaves of the century old trees.

Having lived in the south all of my life, I was feeling as rooted to it as the old trees when suddenly out of the corner of my eye, I caught a glimpse of a mother swallow flopping down out of her porch cornice nest. I thought she'd fallen, but instead she swept quickly out of view to find more food for her nest full of babies. She reminded me of another spring morning when I was photographing quietly in a bird rookery in Southern Florida. With my camera in hand, I watched a Blue Heron spread its wings, then sail silently down to spear a fish. I remembered feeling there for one brief, wonderful moment, the scene and its message frozen in majesty for me. Suddenly the birds, trees, wildflowers, ... even me, were illuminated in a new light, and I realized what an important part we all were of that glorious visual banquet spread out around me that day. I was awed by the beauty of nature that morning and realized for the first time my kinship with all that God had made.

In the next few visits to the swamp, I watched a family of Great Egrets show an almost human quality of love and tenderness to one another. As the family grew and developed I began to understand how closely nature and wildlife parallel human life. First the male and female flew in and out of the trees gathering twigs to build their nests. All the while, the female was preening her feathers and stretching her long graceful neck up and down; and when the male could no longer resist her feminine charms, they mated. After laying her eggs, the female waited patiently for the babies to hatch while the male protected her and brought food. When the chicks were born, both mother and father guarded their home and took turns feeding them. Eventually the time came when the young ones walked out on a limb to stretch their wings, and the parents knew it was time for their fledglings to fly higher and further from the nest. At the same time, other birds and forms of wildlife throughout the habitat were going through a similar cycle: living, fighting, loving, caring, and sometimes, dying, side by side in the community.

I'd thought that each generation of human life had improved upon itself down through the centuries until we'd created the civilization that we know today, but I saw some of the same patterns of living that exist today, there in that bird community. Those weeks in the rookery and other wildlife photography expeditions taught me that many of the basic qualities found in human life are also evident in all life. Love, courage, beauty, simplicity, and solitude are found in nature too, cuddling in the nests, scampering along the grounds, chattering from the branches, soaring above the pond, reaching for the light, or blooming beside the still waters.

The birds, clothed in their beautiful feathers brought so much joy to me, I wanted to share them with others. So I decided to compile some of my photographs into a book. But as I worked, I realized the photographs were not the whole story. While spending so many hours in solitude there in the rookeries, and watching the graceful flight of the egret, my thoughts frequently took wings ... upward toward God, inward toward my true self, and backward toward my spiritual roots. The brief essays I've included in this book are the result of those thoughts as I worshiped in God's cathedral, the world of nature. It is my hope that these pictures and words may inspire you on your own personal journey of looking and reflecting.

So I invite you to come ..., join me for several days in some of these southern swamps, ponds and rookeries. Stand with me as a student at Nature's feet, and perhaps, as they did for Thoreau, visions will open to us, and we'll be better able to see and understand ourselves and our surroundings. Even more important, I think that, as I have done, you too will gain a lifelong friend, — that same "grand, serene, immortal, infinitely encouraging, though invisible, companion[1]" with whom Thoreau walked as we follow the path of "Dancing Feathers."

Tricolored Herons

Roseate Spoonbill

SONG OF SOLITUDE

Great Egret

SONG OF SOLITUDE

H anging vines brushed my face as I quietly approached the sleeping pond. The sun was burning through the foggy morning only to recede back again behind the blanket of misty clouds. Like a choreographer, it directed scattered patches of moving, swaying, drifting light along my path, reminding me of dancers on a stage.

Each time I deliberately set out with my camera knowing there will be days of solitude before me, I feel a terrible loneliness. The loneliness engulfs me. I think of home and the familiar rooms of my life and almost panic at the thought of leaving the ones I love. It's always frightening to be cut away from family and friends. But, "We are all in the last analysis alone," wrote Anne Lindbergh. "Even in a crowd of people we sometimes feel alone. How one avoids it. It seems to imply rejection or unpopularity."[1]

We think we have to keep moving and doing. Our lives are filled with the noise of TV, children wishing to be taken here and there, and the ringing of the telephone. We run errands or go on a trip with family. But, we seldom seek to be alone...to collect our thoughts, to pray, to listen to the sounds of nature, to reflect on where we've been or where we're going. We convince ourselves we do not need solitude. My husband and children need me. I have too many obligations in the community. My mother is ill. My business will fall apart. I have appointments to keep.

It's as if we're afraid of the stillness and quiet. Then, when we've lost our priorities, our inner poise, our balance in life, and the noise suddenly does stop, we wonder with Anne Lindbergh, why "we have no inner music to take its place."[2]

When I finally do pick up my camera and make the break and walk quietly through nature, becoming one with a flower, a leaf, a bird, a butterfly, I discover I haven't given myself up to loneliness at all...but to beauty, to truth, to a symphony being played upon the inner regions of my soul. And there, in the song of the birds, the chirp of the crickets, the touch of a gentle breeze or a caress of falling raindrops, I give myself gladly to the loneliness of solitude in nature. Like Vivienne De Watteville, I exclaim to myself, "How is it possible to feel lonely in one's own element when I am out in Nature. This is the same warm and understanding earth from which I sprang, of which I am composed and to which I shall return; and the trees and flowers and animals and birds are my own blood brother, living together under the same sky warmed and rejoiced by the same sun, loved and redeemed by the same God."[3]

The stillness of the rookery wrapped around me, enfolded me, comforted me. I felt the cool dew-soaked grass beneath my feet as I stood watching the morning light now gloriously shining over the black-silhouetted trees. I no longer felt a loneliness. Instead I felt a freedom of being I'd never experienced before. I watched the Great Egrets with expanded wings circling the pond. There must have been a flock of ten or more. Then the pink Roseate Spoonbills joined them arching together in the sky over the pond. Their Donald Duck bills directed them through the sky like straight arrows. I could hear the sound of their wings like lassos whipping through the air; and soon the black pond was filled with Pelicans, Snowy Egrets, Tri-Colored Herons, and Great Blue Herons. They landed in the black water unafraid and full of glory. It was as though something had signaled them. Suddenly, with a strange energy, everything in the pond began to feed on tiny fish which were making little circles all over the pond. Squawks from the Great Blue Heron and the cackle of a Purple Gallinule and a Common Moorhen joined the sounds of the other birds to penetrate the cool morning air. The activity was almost in a frenzy, and I was surrounded with such great beauty, my heart could hardly hold it.

Fingers of sunlight reached toward the sky as the light gradually expanded from the horizon. I set my camera on the edge of the pond, lifting my tripod high enough to keep an eye on the alligators swimming by. The white wings of birds feeding near me were so close I could almost touch them, but it was as though they were totally unaware of my presence. The wind sang the song of the rookery, not breaking in on the quietness, but "calling up everything to a kind of conscious joy of being." And I was a part of it all, as much a part of the moment as the birds, for I too am a part of nature. The moment was me, distilled, and full of joy. I felt like Vivienne de Watteville when she took her cameras to Africa. "How beautiful is real solitude; "she wrote "not only living in the wilds, but giving yourself up to the spirit that dwells in them."[4]

"Never let me forget this moment," I prayed under my breath to an invisible and mysterious God I knew was there in the stillness of the morning. I wanted the moment to be embedded in my mind so that when my days were once again filled with stress and I had no time for solitude, I could call up this memory and make it mine again.

As the morning became clearer still, some of the birds flew into the surrounding trees. The light cast their shadows all about, and when a breeze suddenly sent the shadows tossing back and forth, the birds wrapped their feet tighter around the limbs and clung steadily there, secure in their place, until they were ready to dive into the dark water and spear a fish. Nature had directed them to the pond where the water was right and the fish were ready to be eaten; and I knew that I too had been directed to the pond. The birds were right for me... the water... the fish... and I knew

I had been sent there out of my need, by a powerful force too great to be seen, to feed on the beauty and solitude.

Finally as the light gave me permission to photograph, I spent my energy selecting the proper lens and seeing one photograph after another appear before me. As I watched the dancing feathers reflect on the water's surface, a Great Blue Heron spread his wide wings, separating himself from the other birds, and flew to the top of a tall pine tree above my head. There was a serenity about the noble figure sitting there alone. His long spear-like bill was lifted to the sky, and he stared out over the pond with a rare dignity. His majestic stance suggested courage and strength and taught me the importance of solitude in my life...that those who wait in quietness will renew their strength...that we will have in our inner being a poise, dignity, serenity and courage to live our lives in greater harmony. But first, like the Blue Heron, we must separate ourselves from the familiarity of life and seek quietness in solitude whether by a pond, near the sea, or in a small cabin on a mountain top.

Slipping the exposed film out of the camera, I could hardly wait for the next day and the adventure that awaited me. I knew I had a lot to learn, but I'd already received a valuable lesson from the pond and its inhabitants that morning. Never again would I let the noise of daily living take over my life. I'd always leave room for God's music to play a song inside of me.

HOLY MOMENTS

Great Egret

Snowy Egret

"Moments of beauty! They are everywhere. They are in every day. You've seen them. You've been in the heart of them."[1] wrote Macrina Wiederkehr. I knew I was in the heart of such a moment as I stood there in the rookery one morning photographing little Snowy Egrets. It was still early. The sun had not yet erased the morning dew. It shimmered on each tiny blade of grass spreading a forest of rainbow colored prisms as far as I could see. The rookery did not lend itself to quietness that morning. It was full of activity...squawking, fighting, feeding, working.

I watched spellbound as a little Snowy Egret lifted out his wings like angel's wings reminding me that "God's incredible gift of the ordinary"[2] in nature, comes to us full of glory when we take the time to be with her. I watched the Egret fly away from his partner and dip down into the water. He hovered there at times like a helicopter fluttering his wings above the pond...dancing and dipping his pointed black bill into the water for fish. Then like a trapeze artist, he suddenly flew up into the air and turned toward the nest trailing his golden slippers behind him. Once he neared the nest, the female curled her long white feathers around her like a graceful ballerina. They created a perfect picture of harmony while I snapped the shutter of my camera over and over again.

The music of the song birds mingled with the noise of the rookery, and I thought, if nature had but one song to sing, each verse would be of beauty. Beauty touches, feeds, strengthens, and energizes our soul. I focused my camera on the little Snowy Egret as he wrapped his yellow slippers around a nearby limb. Nature wraps beauty around us the same way, I thought. Just as the egret's feet embrace the limb, God's beauty embraces us, encourages us, nourishes us. For God is beauty, and when we are in beauty, we know that we are in God. I was in a holy moment.

My heart raced as I gave myself to that moment. Standing there behind the camera, its three legged tripod in place before me, I realized that it is the quality of awareness we give to moments that will "give them the power to bless us." "I will not let you go, O God, unless you bless me,"[3] said Jacob. "I will not let you go, O moment, for you have blessed me," I whispered. I felt enveloped by a symphony as I breathlessly watched the great beauty of the dancing birds on the pond. It was a gift of nature's splendor that I would hold in my heart and make a part of me.

The moments of beauty God gives us each day are like the dew drops, countless and scattered throughout our lives in every direction. As I reached my hand to rest on the tripod, I understood what Macrina Wiederkehr meant when she wrote, "Glory comes streaming from the table of daily life. And Holiness comes wrapped in the ordinary"[4] For the white angel wings of the Egrets, the dewdrops that shimmered across the grass creating a morning of rainbow prisms were ordinary occurrences for the rookery...but for me they were moments of deep and glorious splendor.

The little Snowy Egret and his surroundings were teaching me to look for the hidden holy moments, for the burning bushes in my life; times when God comes wrapped in the every-day common experiences. Jean Bloomcrist wrote, "Seek to be in the embrace of the Holy One by fully encountering each marvelous mundane moment."[5] God had come to me in those ordinary experiences of nature, but I wondered if I would look for God in the ordinary when I got back home. Will I remember when I watch a tiny smile on the face of my grandchild or when I receive a special gift from a family member, I wondered. When a friend calls me on a blue day, or I look into the center of a rose? Will I recognize those moments as holy?

A holy time is not just a morning spent in church taking the sacraments of God, although these things are important to our spiritual life; it is not just the minutes a priest spends asking a blessing for us...those are important, too. But I was learning here in the rookery that a holy moment is any moment spent sensing beauty, listening, praying, loving, and just being...in the presence of God.

The Little Snowy Egret had blessed me that day without even knowing it. We can do that in life for others too, when we are kind, when we remember the goodness of others and ourselves, when we love, when we encourage, when we seek solitude to be present with God...when we see splendor in the ordinary. Yes, all moments are sacred, but I was seeing here in the rookery that it's the quality of awareness we give them, the goodness we see in them, the beauty we feel, the love we express, that makes them holy moments. All of life is sacred if we lend to it Holy thoughts. We will not live in the ordinary; instead if we embrace beauty, we will be like Abraham Hershell who said "Just to be is a blessing, Just to live is Holy."[6]

I would pack my camera and leave the rookery without my shoes, for I knew I had been standing on Holy Ground.

Snowy Egret

KNOW THYSELF

Bald Eagle

Great Egret

I woke up at dawn the next day to get into the rookery before the morning took wing. It was quiet when I reached the pond and the mother Egret was still in her nest. She needs the extra sleep, I thought, with all the work she has to do each day to feed her almost grown-up birds.

Once again I set up my tri-pod, screwed in the camera and lens near the nest, and waited for the right picture. It didn't take long for the mother to wake, stretch, and suddenly take flight with the morning. She moved out of the nest so quickly, I wasn't prepared to snap the picture. As I watched, I saw one of the adolescent birds she'd left behind lift his head over the edge of the nest and try to follow her. He hopped up on one side, lifted one wing, then another, and picked his way through the twigs on the limb.

I had a feeling he was about to fly, and could almost feel him take a deep breath before he made the plunge. Finally, he jumped and, after a flutter or two of his new feathered wings, landed on the ground near me. He hopped about for a few minutes while I sat quietly not daring to move a muscle. I didn't want to interrupt his intense concentration or invade his time of self-discovery. He'd forgotten his brothers and sisters back in the nest and focused so closely on his task of flying...an important part of his truth...that the essence of who he was, was beginning to emerge.

He reminded me of something I'd heard on a trip my husband Roy and I had taken to Greece earlier in the year. We'd traveled from the Ionian Sea, high along the great slope of Mount Parnassus to see the ancient ruins of Delphi. Our guide told us the Greek poet Homolle had called the sight of Delphi "the loveliest in Greece," saying that it "possessed mystery, majesty, and the awesomeness of the divine." I agreed silently as he went on to relate how the priestess of Delphi, dressed in ceremonial robes and holding a laurel branch in each hand, had seated herself on her tripod in the auditorium to pronounce the future and solve the problems of her people.

As we walked and stumbled over the giant stones and columns scattered about the majestic mountain, I wondered what words of wisdom the priestess would pass down through the ages if she were able. As if in answer, our guide said, "The words, 'Know Thyself' are written on one of the cornerstones of Apollo's temple."

It had been hard for me to believe then that something so seemingly simple could be the cornerstone of the ancient Greek's wisdom. And for the first time since we'd left Greece, there in the rookery I found myself once more thinking of those words, "Know Thyself."

I had assumed I knew myself, but did I really? Had I taken the time to know myself as the young bird had done? I never thought there was anything important about knowing myself; and so I'd just accepted life as it came with each decade, without questioning, and somehow the years had seemed to slip away without my even knowing. I had let life absorb me, never taking the time for self-knowledge. Was anything there for me to know, I wondered, as I sat listening to the breeze rustle through the leaves and allowing the stillness of the morning to wash over me. It was calmer in the rookery, easier to think and reflect on those Greek words.

Here in Nature's cathedral, with some distance between me and the other voices and noises I heard each day, I could understand how everyone needs a time such as this...a time to come into harmony with one's self, and let the mind move about in freedom...a time to allow Nature's quiet influence to lead us and bless us. In Isak Dinesen's Letters From Africa, I learned it's easier to be yourself, your whole person, when you're in a new environment, away from all your friends. Perhaps in the separateness, the quietness, and the solitude, here in this rookery, I, too, could go into my own inner resources and discover my real person wrapped up in the folds of my being. Even the young bird had to move away from the other birds before he was able to spread his wings and know his true nature.

Since I'd made family and work my main reason for being, my only ambition, I'd instinctively followed the way of the birds I'd seen in the rookery...working to build the nest and be with my family. In one of her books, my friend Sue Kidd said, "Sometimes I was so busy being tuned into outside ideas, expectations, and demands, I failed to hear the unique music in my own soul.[1]" Hadn't I done that with my own life, I wondered. Not only could I not hear music within; I hadn't even taken time to listen. Another writer wrote, "What gives you bliss? Where does your gladness lie? What gives you zeal and enthusiasm? You are the mystery you seek."[2]

"I am the mystery?" I asked myself. Could this be true? Was this the mystery the Greeks had suggested in searching to Know Yourself? It was hard to believe, but hadn't Jesus said the same thing when he spoke the words, "The Kingdom of God is Within You?"[3] If I'm a mystery I thought...or the kingdom of God is really within me, it seems to me there's nothing much going on there. Often times I'd searched inwardly, never dreaming I was connected to a mystery. All I could see were the problems of daily living; get the pump repaired, cut the shrubs, keep the house together while the remodeling is going on...there's not any mystery in that, I thought...go to the hospital to see a friend, visit elderly relatives, take care of the grandchildren, keep the dust out of the house, be with my husband on his business trips. I was always trying to be aware of the needs of others. After all, wasn't that what a Christian...wife...mother...grandmother...daughter...homemaker...friend should do?

But here in the quiet of the rookery, I could see I'd gotten out of balance and had been confusing my roles in life with who I truly was. By taking the time for self-examination, I realized for the first time that I'd been following Sue's pattern of trying to be all my outside world projected for me to be...the expectation of others, their ideas and demands. I was not hearing any music in my soul. I was too busy trying to be and do all the things others wanted and the things I felt I needed to do. I'd loved my family and friends more than life itself, but where was my bliss? Where was the music? Unable to answer that question there by the still waters, I pulled out my journal to reflect on paper, and probe my inner self for answers...to take the advice of the Greeks and get to "Know Myself."

The first entry in my journal was Vivienne De Watteville's words, "In nature, you learn to know yourself as the thing nearest at hand with whom you must live and work," she wrote, "after which you can forget your very existence in the million beautiful and interesting things around you. And it is the supreme test, because in Nature nothing false can exist. All that is superficial you must shed like a husk, for it has no place there. You are close to life and death, to real things that are fine and sane and simple, and until you have simplified yourself and found out by yourself what is truth for you, you are only on the edge of it."[4]

Alone there in the rookery, I knew I was only touching on the edge of my truth, but I was re-discovering a love for wildness and wild things I'd almost forgotten existed.... I had a feeling it was as much a part of me as flying was a part of the young bird. I began to wonder what other parts were still hidden inside, just waiting for me to search and find them. As I turned another page in my journal, I felt myself connecting again with my roots. I remembered my father and how he'd loved wildlife more than anyone I'd known. He was forever hunting and fishing. I have a photo of him as a young man, taken in the 1920's, wearing laced hunting boots and breeches, and a heavy hunting shirt. It was unbuttoned midway, revealing a white dressy shirt and tie. His snappy-brimmed hat was pushed to one side at a jaunty angle, and he was holding long strings of doves he'd shot. I recalled days we'd spent at the creek where he impatiently threw the line from his rod and reel out into the water again and again. After bringing in the fish, we'd fry them there on the creek bank with other family members. I'd loved those outings and looked forward to them.

Snowy Egret

When he was old and had less energy for hunting and fishing, I'd take him for country outings. I once drove him to Callaway Gardens to see the Spring blooming azaleas. I thought they were lovely, but he never saw the first flower. His only interests were the perch and the bass, their size and number, and whether or not there were people fishing along the scattered lakes. If we were near a field, he'd talk about the habitat of the quail and their breeding colors. He had truly involved his life in nature and followed his bliss.

I laid my journal down in a bed of blooming wildflowers. Colors of yellow, white, and violet spread out around me as I opened the picnic basket I'd brought. Touching a small, star-like, white lily blooming near my feet, I thought of my mother and the happy days of childhood when we picked wildflowers. My mother had followed her bliss, too, but in a different way. She was a gentle person who loved reading and taking long reflective walks. Her Scottish heritage gave a humorous fun-like quality to her individuality. She was also a spiritual person who was deeply committed to her faith. When she was older, there was no need to take her for rides. She was too busy traveling across the country, and to places like Singapore and Australia, counseling and praying with people.

I could see something of myself in parts of my parents; and parts of them, in me. I could even identify with individual characteristics in my aunts, uncles, cousins, and grandparents. These common traits were as much a part of my family and me as flight was a part of the baby Egret here in the rookery. Some might say it was because we all grew up in the same setting and lived by the same basic rules; but I think it was more than environment, more than roots.

Circumstances and surroundings during our childhood play an important role in our development, but I believe, all the major traits that make us who we are, or who we should become, are put there at the moment of creation, embedded in the seed, waiting for us to find them. Sue had said, "Here's where our real selfhood is rooted...in the divine spark or seed, in the image of God imprinted in the human soul. The real self is not our creation but God's. It is the self we are in our depths. It is our capacity for divinity and transcendence."[5]

It was good having nothing to do but let my mind wander among the white clouds and watch their occasional shadows fall across the flowers at my feet. I still couldn't photograph because the light was poor, so as I continued with the journal, another childhood memory of being in wildflowers stretched within my mind and unfolded.

I was four years old. It was 1936, Roosevelt was president, and Jean Harlow was a famous movie star. We were in the deep part of the depression years. My mother, father, brother and I were living with my grandparents in their white Victorian house in middle Georgia. Grandma Moore had two large Magnolia trees in front of the house which my brother and I climbed nearly every day. From one direction I'd look out over her rose garden and in another, I'd see the wide fields of cotton, with patches of wildflowers dotted here and there. I'd think of my favorite fairy tale, Goldilocks and the Three Bears, and daydream for hours in the top of one of those trees pretending I was a hunter like my brother and Daddy.

One morning I got up excited about a hunting trip I'd planned. I put a bow in my bobbed white hair, slipped into my brother's blue overalls, and tried to keep the brass metal from clicking, as I snapped the suspenders over my shoulders. I smelled the pound cake Grandma Moore was baking in the kitchen as I sneaked down the wide brick steps. I was going bear hunting all by myself. I jammed my only weapon, my brother's best sling shot, into my hip pocket, and walked proudly beside Grandma's hen house. My bird dog, Susie Q, joined me as I passed the shed where a syrup kettle nestled in a brick bed built high enough for people to stand around and stir the syrup when the sugar cane was ripe. Then I slipped on down to Daddy's dog pens where I turned out two of his best pointers, Rise and Shine.

The sun was shining, and I felt really free as I passed the tall Sycamore tree at the corner of the old rutted road that led to Grandma's cow pasture. The dogs moved on ahead of me as I marched past the back of the building that housed my grandmother's stick-shift Plymouth and long tongued wagon. I looked past the horse lot into the sprawling barn and could hear the mules and horses grinding and crunching away on their corn. Skipping happily on down the road, I followed the bird dogs past Grandpa's green tenant houses. As the dogs ran on ahead, I started getting scared, but I kept walking on down the road toward the swamp. By the time we got to the pasture, the dogs were out of sight, and I was really scared, not of being alone, but of losing Daddy's dogs. They were scattering and wouldn't answer my call. Nevertheless, I kept going until I came to a wire fence near a wet swampy area that was surrounded with lilies and violets like the ones here in the rookery.

I stood there at the fence feeling my heart in my throat, and called Rise and Shine. Finally I saw them coming. They were barking and growling and tussling with some kind of large furry animal. I quickly loaded the sling shot so that when they reached me, I could give it all the power I had. Suddenly they were in front of me, and I fired away as many times as I dared without killing the dogs too. I was so excited, I was jumping up and down, and crying out in a sing-song voice, "I killed a bear! I killed a bear!" My adrenaline was racing. I was so happy I'd succeeded in killing my game, I didn't hear the sound of footsteps behind me until I suddenly felt a hand on my shoulder and turned to see my tall, straight-backed, stern grandmother.

"What in the world are you doing down here?" she demanded. "I've been looking everywhere for you."

"Grandma," I yelled. "I killed a bear! I killed a bear!" Then I told her the story of my great bear hunt. The moment had electrified me; but she was unimpressed and gave me a whipping I remember to this day.

Because of the way she'd acted, I thought I'd done something terrible. Naturally she'd been afraid I'd get lost in the woods or something bad would happen to me. She'd been right in trying to teach a young child the danger of going to the woods alone, but the experience nonetheless turned me away from hunting and down the path toward a more domestic life. I didn't realize on that long ago morning, in that serendipitous bear-hunting moment, I was actually "following the star of the zeal of my own enthusiasm...following my own bliss."[6]

As I sat there surrounded by the fragrance of deep purple violets, I tried to consciously separate myself from the strong independent nature of that little child still lingering in my memory. She was walking unafraid of outer danger, I thought, feeling only the joy and happiness of being there alone in the swamp. Wasn't that the same spirit I was experiencing again here in the rookery? I shivered as I realized how alive I'd been in those bear hunting moments, those forgotten childhood memories ...and in the present moments nestled among the wildflowers. The superficial part of me was shedding. I was simplifying myself and finding out what was true for me.

Memories came back then, piling quickly, one on top of the other: riding bareback on Stonewall, our blind Shetland pony, and the fun I had when he pulled my brother and me into town on a little green cart painted from leftover tenant house paint; picking violets and wild lilies with my mother and friends on my birthday; swimming in Pappy Jack Springs; the thrill of ballet dancing as a teenager; the hot sunny days when I'd visit my friend, Angela, and we'd talk of writing and singing. What had happened to those interests, those things which had given me joy and excitement? Had I lived such a busy life and involved myself so in the lives of others, that I'd forgotten I had a self? There among the nesting egrets and wildflowers, I resolved not to forget that loving, giving side of me, but I would also start following some of the childhood interests that had given me deep gladness and bliss.

With the journal in hand and still in a contemplative mood, I was discovering threads of truth that had been put in me at my creation, and had remained the same at the age of ten, twenty, thirty, and forty. They had never gone away or changed. I was certain other parts of me were there too, just waiting for me to discover or re-discover them. They would not go away either, in spite of education, influence, circumstances, or surroundings. They might lie buried for a while, but given nourishment they would slip from their bonds to grow and flourish as a Lily unfolds from a bud to form a star. And if I would continue to search for those threads that made me, the "me" I was supposed to be, I'd learn from them to know myself and apply that knowledge to my life. So I decided, there among the hanging vines and deepening shadows, to use the independent, strong will that had been hidden inside me to develop the creative interests that gave me deep gladness. I'd walk in a renewed sense of individuality instead of being caught in the individuality of others.

The shadows of the great trees deepened and fell over the birds and flowers about me. It was time to leave; and as I folded the unused tripod, I could visualize the Greek Priestess from Delphi climbing up on her tripod among the tall columns of the ancient temple to pronounce one of her oracles. Yes, I thought, wisdom had come to the Greeks through the Oracle, but God was teaching me through a little white Egret in this swamp-like rookery.

I walked back toward the car along the snake-like path. As stars began to sparkle through the thick growth of the forest, my steps quickened; not out of fear, but out of some kind of internal rhythm. I knelt beside one of the small pools and touched the long flowing ferns with their prong-like leaves arching over the black water. I smelled the wet loamy earth as I listened to the different tones of music from the roosting birds echoing through the trees. I could feel a presence I'd never felt before. It was like something mystical. Out of the feeling, Dante's words, "I came to myself in the middle of a dark wood"[7] floated through my mind, and I claimed the words for my own truth. I knew I was in a moment I would never forget and that I was finally coming home to my deepest, truest self. In nature, I was myself through and through, "the whole man with God's sigil upon my brow,"[8]...and I knew if I stayed true to this new inner truth, I would be acting out of the will of God for me...out of the music God was playing inside my soul.

Anhinga

Great Egret

FREEDOM OF SURRENDER

Great Egret

FREEDOM OF SURRENDER

After a night's rest, I was back in the rookery in the pre-dawn hours wanting to photograph the birds in that first warm glow of early sunlight. Getting all the equipment in was a chore, but once I was set up, it was like drinking a cup of pure, blissful joy. Back home, I'd always loved photographing my roses in their different stages of bloom, but here in the rookery were flowers that flew, flowers that cried out in anger, flowers that sang ... beautiful flowers with wings. As I set up my tri-pod, I looked back at the dark tree shadows spilling themselves flat over the field behind me, leaving in their wake millions of sparkling dew drops hanging like Christmas ornaments on the stems of the grassy carpet. I was thankful I'd found my way once again to the place that made my heart sing.

I'd been there in the swamp photographing the birds so often by now that anyone else would surely have grown tired of it, but I was only more excited. The Great Egret's fledglings had grown larger and were getting too big for their nest. They were as tall as their mother; and when she flew into the nest, they grabbed her long yellow bill so aggressively they almost overpowered her. Why doesn't she leave the nest, I wondered. Her children are obviously big enough to fly. Even I could see that. The nest was so full of young birds there was no room for THEM, much less the mother; but she would not let go. She'd only come more frequently with her bill filled with food for her grown-up family.

The scene reminded me of my home and the nest I'd left behind. I once had a friend come and visit, and as she looked around our house for the first time, she said, "Janie, you're a true nester." I had been all of my married life. I loved my family and home. They made me happy. Having a home and family had been my only ambition in life. There were eleven years between our oldest and youngest child, with two more children in between, so most of my time and energy had been used in caring for our family.

They were highly energetic children who went through all the stages of growth in a normal happy mode, finishing high school and going off to college. But things began to change when they got older. By the time our youngest son returned from school, the oldest was living next door on our farm, and getting a divorce. Our daughter was also living on the farm with her husband and child. I was often baby-sitting with our only granddaughter. David, our middle son, was deep into a drug problem. I was taking him to A.A. and drug treatment centers while trying to keep family meals going for the swinging door children and retired husband. As if I didn't have enough happening, my husband started a remodeling project that promised to last two years. I was constantly tired and losing control of my life. I felt like the mother bird. Too much was going on in my nest. My life was too full, but the old responsible wife and mother in me was still trying to keep things going at home. I was so divided I could barely function. But what could I do? Like the mother bird, I couldn't just fly away from the nest and leave my family!

There in the rookery watching the collections of birds flying in precision and landing on the glittering light of the pond, I found it easier to collect my thoughts...to concentrate without interruptions. I could see that the frenzy of my life was not natural in nature. There seemed to be rhythms in the life around the pond. Rhythms of growth, of rest, of death and of life. There was strength, poise and patience in nature...Something I hadn't known in years.

As I stood watching the birds fly from one branch to another, I realized the mother wasn't just sitting there in the nest all day like she did when she was hatching the babies. She seemed to be spending more and more of her time searching for greater quantities of food for her grown family. She looked as tired as I was. Her feathers were drooping and she'd lost her beautiful green color around her eyes. Something in me rejected the idea of her weary body out there still getting food for her by-now huge children. I thought about our culture and how it has birthed an ideal human being who must try to be all things to all people. "Do everything! Be everything! Go everywhere!" advertisements scream. Moreover, our spiritual leaders teach us to be all caring, ever giving, ever helpful, anything but being still and learning to "be." Being who you are. We're programmed at every corner of life to be everything someone else wants us to be. I need to be helpful, I thought, especially to my family and friends, but it's almost as if we're asking ourselves to be God to the world.

But that morning in the rookery watching the mother bird I realized I'd been living the same kind of lifestyle, feeding more and more, trying to nurture my grown-up babies. I could see clearly that my problems were similar to the mother bird's problems...the only difference was her children had never gotten out of the nest. Some of my children had already flown away, but I was constantly trying to bring them back again by feeding and helping with all the family situations. I just had not accepted their growth...their individuality. I was still mothering and feeding like the mother bird. They needed to live their own lives and solve their own problems. I was trying to live life for them. Why hadn't I realized before, I wondered, that I really had not learned to let them go. Meister Eckhart wrote that, "For the person who has learned letting go and letting be, no creature can any longer hinder, rather each creature points you toward God and toward new birth and toward seeing the world as God sees it, transparently" and that "When one learns to let go and let be then one is well disposed and he or she is always in the right place whether in society or solitude."[1]

I'd often puzzled over Jesus asking the rich man to give all that he had to the poor when Jesus had made it clear in his teachings that the poor would always be with us. Now I realized it was because He knew the freedom and power the rich man would have in relinquishment. Henry David Thoreau discovered the joy of relinquishment when he gave up home and friends to live alone at Walden Pond. My family and friends were my riches, but I would open my hands and surrender them to be whoever God created them to be. I would let the old mother, wife, sister, child roles in me die. But, wrote Chrissa Pinkola Estes, "What dies? Illusion dies, expectation dies, greed for having it all." Then she said, "We have been taught that death is always followed by more death. It is simply not so, death is always in the process of incubating new life. Even when one's existence has been cut down to the bones."[2] Seeds must die to be born, night must die to make way for a sunrise, and winter must pass away for spring to come..Letting go would be a process; it would not be easy. It would be hard to surrender my control. I really felt afraid to let go. Afraid of change. It had taken me a lifetime of living to become the person I was. To be a part of the family I had. But, I could see in the swamp around me that all of life is change. Life is growth, and death, and being born.

Just as I thought of putting my camera away, I heard one of the large siblings squawking and looked up in time to see the mother egret leading her family out on a heavy limb. I knew it would not be long before they would use their now strong wings to fly out into a new life. It was exciting to think of their lives before them...of the choices they would make, the adventures they would have, the loves, the battles, the failures, the successes. I could see she was finally preparing to let them go...to let them fly away to follow their truths. I felt excited for my family, too, as I resolved within myself to let them go. Not out of my heart for they were too firmly entrenched there...a permanent fixture for all of my days, but out of my control..out of my need to direct their lives.

Then suddenly the mother egret broke away from the younger birds and fluttered through the limbs toward the top of the tree. Then with the help of her wings I saw her weave through the branches until she was standing alone in the very top of the tree. I watched her balanced there, strong and tall, and thought, "yes, she will soon let her fledglings fly away into life's great adventure, to be all that God created them to be. Could I do any less for my family? I asked myself. As I photographed her, I admired her poise and felt her freedom as she lifted her wings in perfect precision, pointed the tips toward heaven, and lifted her full body of feathers off the tree into the soft morning breeze.

The morning light gave way to a sun too harsh to take any more photographs. But just as I'd decided to pack my camera gear and begin my trip home, I saw one of the mother egret's long graceful white feathers floating past me on the lumpy back of an alligator. As the unusual, contrasting scene of light and dark, delicate and rough, moved past me, I took a photograph of it. I wanted to lock the image in my mind to remind me when I got back to Alabama of the lesson learned that day in the rookery. To view again and again, in the hectic days that would surely follow ... the days when I'd forget about my resolution to let go. As the feather slid past me, light and beautiful on the lumpy back of the alligator, I thought, it will remind me too, that I could always return to wild places like this swamp where the wonders of nature will touch my sacred center. That I will find here in the life around me images of God's beauty that will pull the fragmented parts of me back together again.

Picking up my cameras and walking into the beautiful colors of growing things of earth, I felt an inner freedom and deep and powerful love for everything I saw and felt...Perhaps because I had let go, God had given my heart a place to hold all the beauty of His creation in nature. I walked away praying as Vivienne de Watteville had in Africa, "that all this lovely wilderness would not forget me." And she said that the answer was always, "it is not I who will forget, it is for you to find your way back."[3] That is the everlasting message of the Divine through Nature. And because she never intrudes her love upon mankind it is so often passed by unheeded, yet it is there always for anyone who will seek it."

Alligator

Roseate Spoonbills

Come join me now — use your imagination while we wander side by side through the rookery...

Snowy Egrets

Bald Eagle

Great Egret

Gazing on beautiful things acts on my soul, which thirsts for heavenly light.

Michelangelo

Tricolored Heron

Cormorant

The real masters who rule us and rob us of our freedom are indeed within us. They are our own aspirations, feelings, emotions, habits, and passions.

M. Basil Pennington

Great Blue Herons

Osprey

For the person who has learned letting go and letting be, no creature can any longer hinder, rather each creature points you toward God and toward new birth and toward seeing the world as God sees it, transparently. When one learns to let go and let be, then one is well disposed and he or she is always in the right place whether in society or solitude.

Meister Eckart

Snowy Egrets

Tricolored Heron

Nature come streaming into us, wooingly teaching, preaching her glorious living lessons...Here without knowing it, we still were in school; every lesson a love lesson... charmed into us.

John Muir

Tricolored Heron

Great Egrets

*B*ehold you desire truth in the inner
being; make me therefore to know wisdom
in my inmost heart.
        Psalm 51:6, Amplified Bible

White Pelicans

Pelicans, Flamingos, Cormorants

Purple Gallinule

Wood Stork

God writes the gospel not in the Bible alone, but on trees, and flowers, and clouds, and stars.
Martin Luther

Anhinga

White Ibis

Little Blue Herons

When we try to pick out anything by itself, we find it hitched to everything else in the universe. One fancies a heart like our own must be beating in every crystal and cell...

John Muir

Common Moorhen

Common Moorhen

Green-backed Heron

Therefore, I come out to these solitudes, where the problem of existence is simplified. I get away a mile or two from the town into the stillness and solitude of nature,... and it is as if I always met in those places some grand, serene, immortal, infinitely encouraging, though invisible, companion, and walked with him...

Henry D. Thoreau

Wood Stork

Burrowing Owl

Great Blue Heron

Great Blue Heron

CASTING OUR SHADOWS

Great Blue Heron

Great Egret

CASTING OUR SHADOWS

I'd only been home a week from my photography trip to the Florida rookery when Butch Anthony, our young neighbor who worked for my husband on our farm, looked at my pictures and said, "Mrs. Greene, did you know that in June hundreds of those same Egrets and Herons come in to an old pond in Seale?"

"What do you mean?" I asked, hardly believing the glamorous feathered birds could be roosting right here in Russell County...practically in my own back yard.

"It's true," Butch said, "my professor at Auburn told me about seeing a rookery here from a plane, and I went down there last summer to see them. They're about four miles from the farm.... They'll be coming back again soon to lay their eggs and hatch their young chicks."

I prepared all my photography equipment, bought a blind, and a longer lens. Then, when the birds came in, Butch and I, along with Betty and Junior, a couple who also work on the farm, headed for the pond. We drove over slippery clay roads, and stopped about a half mile from the pond. Loaded with tri-pods, cameras, and blinds, we created a trail as we waded through years of leaf mulch and blackberry vines, stumbled over thigh-high rotten logs; oftentimes crunching down to our knees as we struggled with our heavy equipment.

Hot and sweaty, we walked the short distance, and were relieved to finally see a deep shady area. I felt my excitement grow as I heard the sounds of bullfrogs, birds calling their young, mating calls and squawking sounds growing louder and louder. I smelled the damp wet swampy loam as I walked into the deep shade of the thick trees which surrounded the pond. There we stood in a garden of long armed ferns sprawling over the moist earth. The thorn covered vines were so thickly interlaced with the nearby trees they created a solid matt-like wall that concealed the birds. Suddenly my tri-pod caught the thorn covered vines, and sent me sprawling. Pushing ferns out of my face, I called out to the young wildlife enthusiast, "Butch, I don't think our soldiers went through anything rougher than this in Viet Nam."

"Mrs. Greene, people would pay money to come down here and see this," Butch answered without a backwards glance at my arms and legs untangling from the vines. But, as I got back to my feet and looked about me, I had to agree with him, for I felt totally in awe of the strange sounds and beauty of nature that surrounded me there in the darkness of the swamp.

I heard Betty call from a big tangle of vines. She'd found a place to break through to the noisy birds isolated behind the deep wall of vines and trees that surrounded the swamp. While Butch and Junior worked to assemble the tall blind, Betty and I broke through the thick wall of vines. We'd been warned by Butch that one night when he'd been down in the pond, he'd flashed a light on "eighty pair of alligator eyes." So, I balanced myself carefully along a low hanging round branch just inches above the black murky water and yellow blooming water lilies. As Betty carefully held the branches aside for me to push my camera lens into a small opening through the leaves, I looked through my lens and couldn't believe what I saw.

"Great Day in the morning," Betty said. "I ain't never seen anything that beautiful in my life!"

"Betty, I'm almost sick I'm so excited!" I said clicking one photograph after another.

"I'm excited too, Mrs. Greene," she said, "I ain't never been this excited about seeing something. My heart's in my throat!" she said. "I been living here all my life, and I ain't never seem something this beautiful!"

I began snapping pictures of the graceful birds. There were Great Blue Herons, the Little Blue Herons too, Green Backed Herons, and American Bitterns. There must have been 600 Cattle Egrets working frantically building nests. The sun was behind them, and the light caught their puffy brown mating head and wing feathers causing a golden glow around them. When they were flying up and down, out and around, spreading their wide white wings only inches away, they looked like something designed in heaven, they were so pure and beautiful. It was one of those unspeakable moments. The pond was like a virgin world...a mysterious garden...so filled with nature we felt as though we had touched the presence of God!

We completely forgot about the alligators, but as my foot slipped on the limb, I remembered. "Betty," I warned, "Don't forget to climb a tree quick if you see an alligator swim by."

"Don't you worry, Mrs. Greene," she said, "I can climb a tree fast...I can even skinny up one if I need to..." she said, trying to smother her laughter to keep from frightening the birds.

Junior and Butch finally finished the blind, and as they walked up behind us, I heard Junior say, "I remember fishing here at Rye Dawson when I was a little boy."

"Were the birds here then, Junior?" I asked.

"No, ma'am, I ain't never seen nothing like this neither..." he said, pushing his hands down into his pockets and looking reflectively over the pond like a proud African Massi looking over his herd. "But I been fishing here all my days." he said.

"What do you remember about it, Junior?" I asked. "Were there water lilies here?"

"Yes'um, there was a few. It was the blackest water you ever seen. It stayed dark all the time. I lived close by here, and I used to follow my daddy with a stick pole, and we'd catch little fish here. I'd have to run and catch my daddy. One time my daddy ran off and left me down here."

"Why did he leave you, Junior?" I asked out of a lifetime habit of listening to the old stories of the south.

"He was scared of Haints. He was walking along there when something like a Jack-O-Lantern light led him up the road from Rye Dawson Pond. I went on home, and me and Mama heard him hollering. I said it was the devil after him. I couldn't ever see nothing though! He wouldn't ever walk at night after that." Junior said, remembering his childhood.

Before dawn the next morning, dressed in my green camouflage, I was back again at Rye Dawson Pond. I wanted to get some good shots of the Great Blue Herons nesting in the tall dead trees that were protruding eighteen and twenty feet above the black water. I climbed up into the little 4x4 hut-like blind dragging tri-pods and camera lens behind me, hoping I wouldn't drop anything into the dark water below. Trying to be still and quiet and remember not to lean against the wall of cloth camouflage, I set up my tri-pods and cameras and waited for the sun to come up over the quiet pond.

As the sun peeked above the wide gray ribbon of clouds, Rye Dawson and the nesting birds were gradually bathed in the warm glow of the early morning sun. I must have looked like a peeping Tom sitting alone there in the blind, but I had never felt less alone in my life. For while I focused my camera lens on the birds, I was one with them. I remembered Anne Lindbergh's words as she described her feelings about the flying pelicans and sea-gulls in Gift From The Sea. "I felt a kind of impersonal kinship with them," she wrote, "and a joy in that kinship. Beauty of earth and sea and air meant more to me. I was in harmony with it, melted into the universe, lost in it, as one is lost in a cathedral."[1]

From my high perch I watched and listened as the sun brought the pond to life. My senses sharpened to everything around me. A Bullfrog croaked beneath me like a river boat horn in a deep fog. Then, another answered across the pond. The White Egrets were flying over and around me, stealing twigs from the Great Blue Heron's large nest. The giant gray birds flapped their wings and squawked in anger at the

Double-crested Cormorant

little white winged robbers. Other Great Blues sat on distant pine limbs on the swamp`s edge and watched arrogantly over their young fledglings as they stretched in their nest. I snapped one picture after another in the soft morning light.

As the morning lengthened, and the birds grew still, I sat back and thought about my experiences at Rye Dawson. I'd just read one of Emerson's essays, and his words came floating back to me in the quietness of the morning. "All the facts in natural history taken by themselves have no value," he wrote, "but are barren like a single sex. But marry it to human history, and it is full of life."[2] Junior's childhood stories, and the experience of Butch, Betty, and Junior helping me capture the images on film, the shared laughter and story-telling had enabled us to cast our own small shadow of human history over Rye Dawson Pond, too.

No, I thought, I didn't have to go away to the Everglades, even though the Everglades had a unique beauty of it's own. I'd found the birds I'd been looking for in a glade of my own...here in Russell County, in Junior's simple childhood fishing pond...where Jack-O'-Lantern lights once shone, and a child brought his stick pole to dabble away time in the "blackest water you've ever seen." But more importantly, I thought, I'd discovered a deep gladness and a love of beauty in nature that reached my core here in this old pond where the heart of nature throbbed, here among friends in Russell County, at Rye Dawson Pond, a bird rookery...practically in my own back yard.

I had learned one of life's enduring lessons: One need not travel to distant places to find beauty. It is at our finger-tips. The "Dancing Feathers" are right before our eyes, for truly, "earth is crammed with heaven and every common bush aflame with God."

The End

White Ibis

NOTES

In addition to the standard MLA abbreviations, names of people and sources repeatedly cited in these notes are abbreviated as follows:

GFTS   Anne Morrow Lindbergh, *Gift from the Sea,* (New York: Vintage Books and Random House, 1955, 1975)
STTE   Vivienne de Watteville, *Speak to the Earth,* (New York: Viking Penguin, Inc.,1986)
ATFA   Macrina Wiederkehr, *A Tree Full of Angels,* (New York: HarperCollins Publishers, 1988)
LFA   Isak Dinesen, *Letters form Africa,* (Chicago: University of Chicago, 1981). Originally published as BREVA FRA
        AFRIKA 1914-24 (Rungstedlundfonden, 1978)
THJ   Joseph Campbell, *The Hero's Journey,* (New York: HarperCollins Publishers, 1990)
MME   Matthew Fox, *Meditations with Meister Eckart,* (Santa Fe, NM: Bear and Company, 1983)
WEA   Sue Monk Kidd, "Birthing Compassion," *Weavings* 5, (Nov-Dec. 1990)

NATURE'S PATTERNS

1.   Henry David Thoreau.

SONG OF SOLITUDE

1.   GFTS, 41-42.
2.   GFTS, 42.
3.   STTE, 274.
4.   STTE, 316.

HOLY MOMENTS

1.   ATFA, 29.
2.   ATFA, xiii.
3.   Holy Bible, Genesis 32:26
4.   ATFA, xiii.
5.   Jean Blomquist, "Daily Dancing with the Holy One," *Weavings* 6, (November/December 1989):12.
6.   Matthew Fox, *Original Blessing,* (Santa Fe, NM: Bear & Co. Inc., 1983) 42.

KNOW THYSELF

1.   WEA, 23.
2.   THJ, xiv, xv, 65.
3.   Holy Bible, Luke 17:21.
4.   STTE, 274.
5.   WEA, 26.
6.   THJ, xiv.
7.   Dante, "The Divine Comedy."
8.   LFA, 376.

FREEDOM OF SURRENDER

1.   MME, 55, 63.
2.   Clarissa Pinkola Estes, Ph.D., *Women Who Run with the Wolves,* (New York: Random House, Inc., 1992) 135,140.
3.   STTE, 193.

CASTING OUR SHADOWS

1   GFTS, 43.
2.   Ralph Waldo Emerson, *Nature* (Boston: Beacon Press).

QUOTES ON PHOTOGRAPHS IN ORDER OF APPEARANCE

1.   Michelangelo.
2.   M. Basil Pennington, O.C.S.O., *Thomas Merton, Brother Monk.* (San Francisco: Harper & Row, Publishers, 1987) 21.
3.   MME, 55, 63.
4.   ed. Peter Browning, *John Muir In His Own Words* (Lafayette, CA: Great West Books) 68.
5.   Amplified Bible, Psalm 51:6
6.   Martin Luther.
7.   ed. Peter Browning, *John Muir In His Own Words* (Lafayette, CA: Great West Books) 12.
8.   Henry David Thoreau.

*L*et be and be still, and know - recognize and understand - that I am God! I will be exalted in the earth!